Understanding the Australian Age Pension Means Tests

A Practical Guide to Understanding Income and Assets Tests

Dan Whitmore

pensionwhy

This publication is intended for educational and informational purposes only and is designed to assist readers in understanding the Australian Age Pension Means Tests and related assessment concepts.

The Australian Age Pension system, legislation, rates, thresholds, and assessment rules discussed in this publication are derived from publicly available information published by the Australian Government and may change over time.

This book represents the author's interpretation, explanation, and educational presentation of those concepts and does not constitute financial advice, legal advice, taxation advice, or personal advice.

Readers should consider their individual circumstances and confirm current requirements with the relevant government authorities or seek professional advice before making financial or retirement planning decisions.

First Edition: 2026

Published by pensionwhy

ISBN: Paperback 978-1-7648104-0-1

Contents

Introduction

For many Australians, the Age Pension represents more than just a fortnightly payment. It provides financial support, stability and peace of mind during retirement. Yet, despite its importance, the Age Pension system can often feel confusing and overwhelming.

Some worry that they may not qualify for the Age Pension because they have savings or own investments. Others are unsure about how their income and assets are assessed, or whether changes in their circumstances could affect their payments. Many simply want to understand the rules so they can make informed decisions with confidence.

What became clear to me is that much of the confusion does not arise because the rules are impossible to understand. Rather, the information is often scattered across lengthy guides, legislation and official publications that can be difficult to navigate. As a result, many people are left uncertain about their entitlements or anxious about making mistakes.

This book was written to help bridge that gap. The purpose of this book is to explain, in plain English, how the Australian Age Pension Means Tests operate. In particular, it focuses on the rules surrounding income, assets, deeming, gifting and other common areas that frequently affect Age Pension entitlements.

This book is intended for current Age Pension recipients, people approaching retirement, family members assisting older Australians, and anyone who wishes to gain a clearer understanding of how the Age Pension Means Tests work.

While every effort has been made to ensure that the information presented is accurate and easy to understand, it is important to remember that social security rules change regularly and individual circumstances differ. This book should therefore be used as an educational resource and general guide rather than a substitute for professional advice or official government information.

My hope is that, by the end of this book, you will feel more confident in understanding the Age Pension

Means Tests, better equipped to identify issues that may affect your entitlements, and more comfortable navigating what can sometimes seem like a complex system.

Retirement should be a time of greater certainty and peace of mind. Understanding how the Age Pension rules apply to your circumstances is an important step towards achieving that confidence.

Chapter 1: The Residency Threshold — Is Australia Your Home?

When people start looking into the Age Pension, their minds almost immediately jump to the "means tests." They think about their bank accounts, their investments, and the value of their family home. That is understandable—the financial side of the pension is complex and often intimidating. However, there is a quiet, foundational rule that sits at the very front of the process. If you don't cross this threshold, the financial calculations that follow become irrelevant. That gatekeeper is the residence requirement.

Before the government ever asks you about your savings, they need to verify one fundamental question: Is Australia your home?

The Triple Test

You cannot simply claim the pension because you have reached the qualifying age. On the specific day you lodge your claim, you are legally required to meet three criteria simultaneously. It is a "triple test" of your connection to the country.

First, you must be living in Australia. Second, you must be physically present in Australia. Third, and perhaps most importantly, you must be an "Australian resident."

While those first two conditions seem straightforward, the term "Australian resident" acts as a specific legal definition within the social security framework. You don't need to hold a particular job or own a property to qualify, but you must fall into one of three distinct categories:

- You are an Australian citizen.
- You hold a permanent visa.
- You are a protected Special Category visa (SCV) holder—essentially, certain New

Zealand citizens who were present in Australia under specific conditions.

If you don't fit into one of these three buckets, you simply do not meet the primary residence status required to lodge a valid claim.

Defining "Residing"

It is common for applicants to assume that holding the right visa or citizenship is the end of the conversation. In reality, it is only the beginning. The government goes a step further to determine whether you are actually "residing" in the country. This is where the subjective nature of the assessment kicks in.

The authorities don't just look at where you sleep at night; they look at the "big picture" of your life to determine if your settled, usual place of abode is in Australia. They evaluate your connection to the country through six specific lenses:

1. Travel Patterns: How often do you leave, and for how long? Frequent or extended absences can signal that your life is centred elsewhere.
2. Accommodation: What is the nature of the housing you occupy while in Australia? Is it a transient arrangement, or is it a stable home?
3. Family Ties: Where are your immediate family members located? Strong domestic family ties suggest deeper roots in the country.
4. Economic Ties: This covers the nature and extent of your employment, business interests, and financial life.
5. Assets: The location of your significant assets serves as a proxy for where you intend to manage your long-term affairs.
6. Intent: Finally, they consider any other matter that helps paint a clear picture of your intention to remain here permanently.

There is no "magic number" of factors you need to tick. Instead, it is a holistic view. It is an exercise in proving that your life, your interests, and your future are firmly anchored to Australian soil.

The Ten-Year Commitment

Even if you satisfy all the residency status requirements and have firmly established that Australia is your home, you must still contend with the clock. The social security system requires a significant, long-term commitment to the country before you become eligible for age-related support.

Generally speaking, you must have been an Australian resident for at least 10 years in total[1]. This isn't just a cumulative calculation, however. To ensure that your residency isn't merely historical, the government imposes a continuity rule: at least five of those years must be a continuous period, without a significant break.

Think of it as a decade-long demonstration of residency. The government wants to see that you have lived here as a member of the Australian community for a substantial portion of your later life. If you have

---

[1] Excludes special qualification pathways under International Social Security Agreements, refugee/humanitarian exemptions, or specific provisions for widowed residents.

moved back and forth between countries, or if your residence has been fragmented by long periods abroad, you may find that you fall short of this 10-year threshold.

If you haven't reached that decade of residence, your application will likely hit a wall before the means tests even begin. Understanding this requirement is essential, as it highlights that the Age Pension is designed for those who have spent a meaningful portion of their lives contributing to and living within the Australian framework. Once you have cleared this decade-long hurdle, and only then, are you ready to open the books and begin the complex process of the means tests.

Chapter 2: The Relationship Status — Defining the "Couple"

Once you have established that you meet the residency requirements, the next major pivot point in your application is your relationship status. This might sound like a simple question of "single" or "married," but in the world of social security, it carries significant financial weight. Because the Age Pension is designed as a safety net, the government assesses your financial position—and that of your partner—as a unit. This is why getting your status right is just as important as having your residency papers in order.

The Financial Distinction

The government pays different rates depending on your relationship status. The fundamental logic is that couples living together share the costs of daily life—housing, utilities, and groceries—meaning their combined needs for support are different from someone living alone.

However, the system also recognises that your circumstances may prevent you from living together. If you and your partner are separated due to ill health, you are essentially treated as two single individuals for payment purposes, as your living expenses are effectively doubled.

The maximum payment rates—which include the base pension, pension supplement, and energy supplement—are structured as follows:

Status	Maximum payment per fortnight
Single	$1,200.90
Member of couple (each)	$905.20
Couple apart due to ill health (each)	$1,200.90

Note: These figures are current and valid as at March 2026.

Who is a "Member of a Couple"?

For the purpose of your pension, the definition of a "member of a couple" is broader than just those who are legally married. You are considered a member of a couple if you are in a relationship with another person as their partner and are not living separately and apart on a permanent or indefinite basis. This includes three main categories:

- Legally Married: You are in a union that is recognised under the Marriage Act.
- Registered Relationship: You are in a relationship registered under a State or Territory law, often referred to as a civil union or partnership.
- De Facto Relationship: You are in a relationship as a couple on a genuine domestic basis.

The "Big Picture" Assessment

If the nature of your relationship is ever in question, the government performs a holistic assessment to determine whether you and another person are genuinely living as a couple or single (separated under one roof). There is no single factor that, on its own, decides this; rather, it is the weight of all the evidence taken together.

When making this determination, the authorities look at five primary areas:

1. The financial aspects of your relationship.
2. The nature of your household.
3. The social aspects of your relationship.
4. The sexual relationship between you and your partner.
5. The nature of your commitment.

When Relationships Change

Sometimes, your circumstances change. Perhaps you and your partner have physically separated, or perhaps you remain under the same roof but are now living entirely separate lives due to an emotional breakdown in the relationship.

Crucially, the government acknowledges that people can be "living separately and apart" even if they are still sharing a home. This is often the case when a relationship has ended but, due to the cost of moving out or other pressures, one party cannot move out immediately. However, simply living in separate rooms is not enough; there must be a genuine, permanent, or indefinite breakdown in the relationship.

Chapter 3: Homeowner or Non-Homeowner? — The Residence Divide

Once you have cleared the initial hurdles of residency and relationship status, you reach a vital classification phase. Before any financial calculations occur, the social security system must determine your status as either a "homeowner" or a "non-homeowner." This classification is a foundational element of how your situation is assessed.

Defining the Homeowner

According to the *Social Security Guide (4.6.3.20)*, you are classified as a homeowner if you—or your partner—have a right or interest in the place you occupy, and that right or interest grants you "reasonable security of tenure." This means you have a legal or recognised basis to remain in your home.

You are generally regarded as a homeowner if you reside in:

- A home owned or partly owned by you or your partner.
- A residence to which you hold legal title.
- A home owned by a company, provided that company grants you reasonable security of tenure.
- A campervan, caravan, transportable home, or boat owned or partly owned by you or your partner, in which you have reasonable security of tenure.
- A "special residence" that meets the specific requirements for special residences.

Selling Your Home: The 24-Month Rule

A common point of confusion is what happens to your status after you sell your principal home. The system recognises that selling and moving is a process that takes time, so your status as a "homeowner" does not automatically disappear the moment the property is sold.

You continue to be assessed as a homeowner if you have sold your principal home and:

- You intend to use some or all of the proceeds to purchase, build, rebuild, repair, or renovate a new principal home within 24 months from the date of sale.
- You have already applied some or all of the proceeds to build, rebuild, repair, or renovate a new principal home within that 24-month window.

There is also a provision for an extension. If you have been unable to complete your plans within 24 months, you may still be classified as a homeowner for up to 36 months if you continue to meet the requirements to gain an extended exemption. This includes demonstrating a continuing intention to use the proceeds for a new principal home and showing that delays—such as building approval issues, health-related hospitalisations, or professional delays in the building industry—were beyond your control.

When You Become a Non-Homeowner

Conversely, you will be classified as a non-homeowner if you cannot be defined as a homeowner under the criteria above. According to the *Social Security Guide (4.6.3.20)*, you are a non-homeowner if you:

- Have sold your principal home in the last 24 months but do not intend to use the proceeds to purchase, build, repair, or renovate a new home in the next 24 months.
- Have sold your principal home and have not used the sale proceeds to purchase, build, repair, or renovate a new home within 24 months (and did not meet the criteria for an extended exemption).

Understanding these transitions is essential. Your status is not just a label; it defines how the system views your housing security and, by extension, how it will eventually apply the means tests to your financial profile.

Chapter 4: Defining Your "Principal Home"

Now that we have established your status as either a homeowner or a non-homeowner, we need to address exactly which property qualifies as your "principal home." In the social security system, your principal home is generally an exempt asset, meaning its value is not counted when determining your pension eligibility. Defining this property correctly is essential, as it dictates what is shielded from the assets test.

The General Rule

According to the *Social Security Guide (4.6.3.30)*, your principal home is generally the residence in which you—as a single person or as part of a couple—live for the greatest amount of time each year.

If you or your partner owns more than one home, the rules are straightforward:

- Time Spent: The principal home is the one in which you spend the greatest amount of time.
- Equal Time: If you spend an equal amount of time in each, the most expensive property is defined as the principal home.
- If you spend a significant amount of time living in a home that you do not own (such as staying with relatives), the home you do own remains your principal home.

Self-Contained Living Areas

The rules become more nuanced when a property includes a self-contained living area—a space with its own private sleeping, cooking, and bathroom facilities. Whether this area is considered part of your principal home (and therefore exempt) depends on its use:

- Vacant: It is treated as part of your principal home.
- Let to a near relative: It is treated as part of your principal home.

- Let to another person: It is not part of your principal home and is considered an assessable asset.

Temporary Absence from Your Home

Life is rarely static, and the system accounts for times when you may need to leave your home temporarily. Under the *Social Security Guide (4.6.3.60)*, an absence is generally regarded as temporary unless you state a definite intention never to return.

The length of time your home remains an exempt asset during a temporary absence depends entirely on the reason for your departure:

- Entering a Care Situation: If you vacate your home to enter a care situation (such as moving into an aged care facility), your principal home can continue to be treated as an exempt asset for up to 24 months.
- Caring for Another Person: If you are absent from your principal home to provide substantial care to another person in a private

residence, your home can be treated as an exempt asset for up to 24 months.

- Loss or Damage to the Principal Home: If your home is lost or damaged, the property can continue to be considered your principal home for up to 12 months while you undertake repairs or rebuilding. This period can be extended up to 24 months if you have made reasonable attempts to rebuild or repair the home and have experienced delays beyond your control (such as building industry shortages or other factors you could not influence).
- Other Reasons: For other temporary absences, such as travelling around Australia or overseas, the home generally remains an exempt asset for up to 12 months.

If your absence exceeds these timeframes, or if you decide during your absence that you have no intention of returning, your principal home will lose its exempt status and become an assessable asset. At that point, you may be reclassified as a non-homeowner, to which the higher non-homeowner allowable assets threshold applies.

Chapter 5: Rent Assistance — Helping with Housing Costs

For those who do not own their home, the costs of housing—whether it be rent, lodging, or site fees—can be a significant burden. The government provides a supplement called "Rent Assistance" to help eligible pensioners cover these costs. If you are already receiving an Age Pension, you may be eligible for this additional payment, provided your housing costs reach a certain threshold.

Who Can Receive Rent Assistance?

Rent Assistance is a non-taxable, fortnightly payment available to many income support recipients. To qualify, you generally need to be receiving the Age Pension and paying "rent" for your principal home. In the eyes of the system, "rent" is broadly defined. It doesn't just mean paying a landlord for a private rental house or apartment. You may also be eligible if you pay:

- Lodging or board and lodging.
- Fees to a retirement village if classified as a non-homeowner.
- Fees for a site or mooring for a caravan, relocatable home, or boat that you use as your principal home.

However, you are generally ineligible if you:

- Own or are buying the home you live in.
- Live in a government-funded residential aged care facility.
- Lease a property from a state or territory housing authority (as these rents are already subsidised).

How Much You Can Receive

The amount of Rent Assistance you receive is determined by the amount of rent you pay. The system uses a sliding scale: once your fortnightly rent exceeds a set minimum "rent threshold," you receive 75 cents for every dollar of rent you pay above that amount, up to a maximum payment limit.

If you are	Your fortnightly rent is more than	To get the max payment your fortnightly rent is at least	The maximum fortnightly payment is
single	$154.80	$447.34	$219.40
single, sharer	$154.80	$349.83	$146.27
couple, combined	$250.80	$526.54	$206.80
one of a couple separated due to illness	$154.80	$447.34	$219.40
one of a couple temporarily separated	$154.80	$430.54	$206.80

Note: These figures are current and valid as at March 2026.

A Note on Board and Lodging

It is common for pensioners to live in arrangements where they pay for both their accommodation and meals—commonly known as "board and lodging." Because Rent Assistance is strictly for housing, the government only counts the portion of your payment that relates to lodging.

If your agreement clearly distinguishes how much you pay for room (lodging) and how much for food (board), that specific lodging amount is used to calculate your assistance. However, if you are unable to identify exactly how much you pay for the lodging component, the system applies a standard "two-thirds rule." Under this rule, two-thirds of the total amount you pay for combined board and lodging is treated as the rent component for the purpose of calculating your assistance.

How to Access the Payment

One of the most helpful features of this system is that you generally do not need to lodge a separate application. If you have already claimed the Age Pension and provided details about your living arrangements, the department will automatically assess your eligibility for Rent Assistance. Should your circumstances change—such as moving house, starting to pay rent, or a change in your board and lodging costs—you simply need to update your details with them, and they will adjust your payments accordingly.

Chapter 6: Principal Home on Large Land (Over 2 Hectares)

For most Australians, the principal home is an exempt asset. However, when your home sits on a large block of land—specifically, land exceeding 2 hectares on a single title—the rules become more nuanced. In these cases, the social security system must distinguish between the land used for your private, domestic life and any remaining land that may be considered an assessable asset.

The Private Land Use Test

As a starting point, the "Private Land Use Test" applies to all income support recipients. Under this rule, your principal home and the surrounding 2 hectares of land on the same title document are generally exempt from the assets test, provided they are used primarily for private or domestic purposes in association with your dwelling.

If your land is larger than 2 hectares, the "excess" land is typically counted as an assessable asset. For example, if your home is situated on 6 hectares of land held on a single title, the first 2 hectares are exempt, while the remaining 4 hectares are included in your assets test, and their market value will be assessed accordingly.

The Extended Land Use Test

Recognising that rural customers and primary producers may have unique circumstances, the government provides an "Extended Land Use Test" for Age Pensioners. This rule allows for the possibility of exempting all the land on your title, even if it exceeds 2 hectares, provided specific criteria are met.

To qualify for this exemption, you must satisfy the following according to the *Social Security Guide (4.6.8.50)*:

- Age and Qualification: You must have reached Age Pension age and be qualified for the Age Pension.
- Long-Term Attachment: You must have had a long-term, continuous attachment to the principal home and the land for 20 years or more. For couples, at least one member must meet this 20-year attachment requirement.
- Effective Use of the Land: You must be making "effective use" of the productive land.

What is "Effective Use"?

"Effective use" is a core requirement for the extended exemption. It is generally satisfied if you are using the land to its potential to generate income or if the land has limited to no potential to generate income. You may satisfy this requirement if:

- You are working the land: You, or a family member, are running a farming business on the land.
- Leasing the land: You are leasing the land to others for a commercial rate of return.

- No potential to earn: The land is not being used because it truly has no, or very limited, potential to generate income.

Conversely, you will generally not satisfy the test if you are working productive land but not to its potential, or if you are not working productive land that has clear income-generating capacity.

Exclusions and Considerations

It is critical to understand that even if you qualify for the Extended Land Use Test, the exemption applies only to the land. It does not extend to commercial or business assets, such as:

- Machinery, plant, or specialised equipment.
- Livestock or stock-in-trade.

These items remain assessable assets regardless of whether the land itself is exempt. Furthermore, if you use a specific portion of your principal home or its surrounding land *solely* for business purposes—such as a dedicated home office, a commercial workshop, or a storage facility—that specific part of the property is excluded from the home exemption and will be counted as an asset.

Chapter 7: The Foundation of the Means Tests — Income and Assets

You have successfully navigated the "gatekeeper" rules: residency, relationship status, homeownership, and property aspects. You are now standing at the doorway of the means tests themselves. To understand how your Age Pension is calculated, you must first understand the two distinct lenses the government uses to view your financial life: the Income Test and the Assets Test.

Every piece of property, money, or earnings you have is categorised into one of these two buckets. Often, an asset can generate income (like a bank account generating interest), meaning it can be assessed under both tests simultaneously.

What is "Assessable Income"?

Income for pension purposes is much broader than just your salary or wages. The government looks at the money coming into your household from almost every source. This includes, but is not limited to:

1. Employment Income: Wages, salaries, and commissions, including those earned by your partner.
    a. Fringe Benefits: The non-grossed-up value of benefits provided by an employer.
    b. Salary Sacrifice: Even if you choose to redirect salary into superannuation or other benefits, these amounts are generally included as assessable income for social security purposes.
    c. Director's Fees: Any payments received for your role as a director.
2. Financial Investments: This is where the "deeming" system comes in. Rather than looking at the actual interest you earn, the government assumes your financial assets earn a set rate of return.

3. Rental Income: Money you receive from renting out a property (including a former principal home or a self-contained unit on your current property).
4. Income from boarders and lodgers who aren't immediate family members.
5. Income from a sole trader or partnership business.
6. Income from a farm.
7. Foreign Income: Any pension or earnings you receive from outside Australia.
8. Private Trusts and Companies: If you have control or an interest in a private trust or company, the income generated by those structures may be attributed to you.
9. Pay to a member of the Australian Defence Force Reserve for continuous full-time service.
10. Certain scholarship amounts.
11. Some lump sums.

The Two Categories of Lump Sum Income

When you receive a large, one-off payment, it is crucial to understand that it is classified into two specific categories for assessment purposes:

1. Remunerative Lump Sums: These are payments linked to work or employment. They are counted as income from the date they are received for the length of time to which they relate.
    - *Example:* If you receive a commission or bonus payment that covers a 3-month period of work, that amount is assessed as income for those 3 months.
2. Non-Remunerative Lump Sums: These are one-off or irregular payments that are not linked to work or employment. These are generally counted as income and apportioned over a 52-week (12-month) period from the date you become entitled to receive them.
    - *Example:* Distributions from a family trust or dividends from a private company are generally treated as

non-remunerative and spread across 52 weeks to determine your income for those weeks.

The "Lump Sum" Factor

A common point of confusion is how lump sums are treated. If you receive a large, one-off payment—such as a superannuation withdrawal, a payout from a deceased estate, or a windfall—it is generally treated as a shift in your asset profile. Once that money hits your bank account, it becomes a financial asset and will be subject to deeming. It is not necessarily "income" in the sense of a salary, but it will affect your assets test and, through the deeming process, your income test.

What Doesn't Count in the Income Test

Lump sums may be exempt from the income test if they meet all of these:

- Unlikely to happen again.
- Hard to predict.
- Not for a service or work provided.

They include any of these:

- A one-off gift, prize, reward, lottery win, or amount of superannuation.
- An inheritance.
- A payout from a property settlement, or for damages to property or personal effects.
- Flood, bushfire and drought assistance.
- Some redress payments, such as for negligence.
- Compensation from an Australian trust.

What are "Assessable Assets"?

When the government asks for your "assets," they are looking for the current net market value of everything you own or have an interest in. This is the amount you could reasonably expect to get if you sold the item on the open market today, minus any debts (like a mortgage) secured against it.

1. Financial Investments: Bank accounts, term deposits, cash on hand, shares, managed investments, money loaned, money held in solicitor trust accounts, bonds and debentures, gold, silver or platinum bullion.

2. Real Estate: Any property other than your exempt principal home. This includes holiday homes, vacant land, and the "excess" land on your principal home title (if it exceeds 2 hectares).
3. Business Assets: If you are a sole trader, in a partnership, or control a private company or trust, the value of those business structures is assessed.
4. Annuities, income streams and superannuation: If you have reached Age Pension age, your superannuation (even in the accumulation phase) is counted as an asset.
5. Gifting: If you give away assets for less than their market value (above certain thresholds), those "gifts" may still be counted as your assets for five years.
6. Home contents, personal effects, vehicles and other personal assets.
    - Household contents such as furniture and appliances.
    - Personal Effects: jewellery, laptops, and collections (like stamps or coins).
    - Vehicles: Cars, boats, and caravans.

- Licences: commercial fishing and taxi.
- Insurance policies: surrender value of life insurance policies.
- Cryptocurrency and other cryptocurrency assets.

What is Exempt?

The most significant exempt asset is your principal home. Others include:

- Prepaid funeral expenses and funeral bonds (up to certain limits).
- An accommodation bond paid to an aged care facility.

How They Work Together

It is important to remember that the government applies both the income test and the assets test to your situation.

- The Income Test focuses on your "flow" of money.

- The Assets Test focuses on your "stock" of wealth.

Accurately reporting income and assets ensures that the department can calculate and apply the correct pension rate. In cases where the classification of an income and asset source is ambiguous, declaring the item allows the department to make the formal determination. The system is designed to be comprehensive; by understanding these foundational categories, you are now prepared to dive into the specific calculations that determine your fortnightly payment.

Understanding the Mechanics

It is vital to recognise that the government is looking for your total financial capacity. If you move money from a savings account into an investment property, your classification shifts from "financial asset" (subject to deeming) to "real estate" (subject to market valuation).

If you are part of a couple, it does not matter whose name the asset is in or who earned the income; the government assesses your financial position jointly. This holistic approach ensures that your pension rate reflects your household's total resources, not just the money held in your individual name.

Chapter 8: Navigating the Means Tests — Income and Assets Limits

To ensure government support is directed where it is most needed, the system employs a dual-purpose framework: the income test and the assets test. These mechanisms establish "free areas"—thresholds within which your financial resources have no impact on your payment rate. Beyond these limits, your payment is gradually reduced as your resources increase.

The Income Test

The income test assesses how your earnings from various sources affect your fortnightly payment. If your income exceeds the "income free area," your payment is reduced by 50 cents for singles, and 25 cents for couples (each).

Status	Income free area	Income limit
	Per fortnight	
Single	$226	$2,627.80
Couple combined	$396	$4,016.80
Illness separated,	$396	$5,199.60

Note: These figures are current and valid as at July 2026.

The Assets Test

The assets test examines the total value of your assets to determine your eligibility and payment rate. For every $1,000 of assets over the assets free area, your pension payment is reduced by $3.00 per fortnight.

Status	Assets free area	Assets limit
	Homeowner	
Single	$333,000	$733,500
Couple combined	$499,000	$1,102,500
Illness separated	$499,000	$1,300,000
	Non-homeowner	
Single	$600,000	$1,000,500
Couple combined	$766,000	$1,369,500
Illness separated	$766,000	$1,567,000

Note: These figures are current and valid as at July 2026.

Understanding Cut-off Points

The "cut-off point" refers to the specific level of income or assets at which your payment rate reduces to nil. By familiarising yourself with these thresholds, you can gain a clearer picture of how your financial situation aligns with the support available.

Chapter 9: Employment Income

Assessing Employment Income: When is it Counted?

Understanding when your employment income is assessed is crucial for maintaining accurate records and ensuring your payment support remains consistent. A fundamental principle of the social security system is that employment income is assessed once it is paid by an employer to their employee.

The Point of Payment

Employment income is typically considered "paid" on the specific date recorded by your employer as the pay day. Employers are required to provide a payslip that clearly states the date the payment was made, which serves as the reference point for assessment.

It is important to note the following regarding the timing of this assessment:

- Bank Processing Delays: If there is a delay between when your employer processes the payment and when the funds actually reach your bank account (for example, due to bank transfer times), the income is still considered paid on the date recorded as the official pay day.
- Early Deposits: If your employer disburses funds to your bank account before the official pay date, the income is still assessed based on the pay day recorded on your payslip and within Single Touch Payroll (STP) data.
- Employment Relationship: This "assessed when paid" rule applies specifically to remunerative work undertaken as an employee within an employer/employee relationship. Other forms of income, such as self-employment income, are generally assessed when first earned, derived, or received.

Examples

Example 1: Michael is paid by his employer each Wednesday, but his employment income does not arrive in his bank account until Thursday. Michael's employer records his pay day as Wednesday, so Michael's employment income is taken as paid on Wednesday. *Social Security Guide (4.3.3.05)*

Example 2: John collects his wages from his employer in cash. His employer calculates the wages and makes the income available on Thursday, but John does not collect his income until his next shift on Saturday. John's employment income is taken as paid on Thursday. *Social Security Guide (4.3.3.05)*

Preventing Manipulation

The policy of assessing income when it is paid—rather than when it is received—is designed to prevent incentives for individuals to manipulate the system. Specifically:

- It discourages employees from deferring the receipt or collection of their pay (such as delaying the provision of bank details) to gain an advantage.

- If the payment of employment income is intentionally deferred to obtain a social security advantage, the Secretary may determine that the income was assessable at the time the decision to defer was made.

By aligning the assessment with the official pay date, the system maintains a fair and consistent approach for all recipients.

Attributing Employment Income: The Employment Period

When assessing employment income for social security purposes, it is not always enough to simply look at the date a payment was made. To ensure fairness and accuracy, the system uses the concept of the employment period to determine when income was actually earned and to which period it should be attributed.

Defining the Employment Period

According to the *Social Security Guide (4.3.3.06):* For wages and salaries, the employment period is typically the length of the employer's pay cycle or an income support payment entitlement period, whichever is longer. For other types of income, such as commissions or bonuses, the employment period will be the total period of time over which the amount was earned.

Determining the Assessment Period

To ensure that your income is accurately accounted for, the system utilises an assessment period to link your earnings to your specific social security reporting cycle. This process is essential for maintaining consistency, particularly when your employment cycle does not perfectly align with the standard fortnightly reporting period.

Defining the Assessment Period

The assessment period is the period of time for which a person is required to report their income for social security purposes. For income support payments like Age Pension, this is a 14-day period.

When assessing your employment income, the department looks at the income you were paid during this assessment period, regardless of when that work was actually performed.

Key Rules for Assessment

The following guidelines are used to determine which income is counted during your assessment period:

- Payment Timing: Employment income is generally assessed in the assessment period in which it is paid to you.
- Multiple Payments: If you receive more than one payment of employment income within a single assessment period, all those payments are added together and assessed for that specific 14-day cycle.

- Exceptions: There are specific circumstances—such as when employment income is paid in advance or arrears, or when the payment covers a period longer than the assessment period—where the department may use different methods to attribute that income to ensure a fair assessment.

Why This Matters

By utilising a defined assessment period, the system creates a clear, predictable framework for both the recipient and the department. It ensures that your payment rate for each fortnight is based on a consistent assessment of your paid income, helping to avoid complexities when pay cycles and reporting cycles overlap.

By understanding how these periods are structured, you can better manage your income reporting and anticipate how different pay schedules might affect your fortnightly payments.

Examples

Example 1: Jess is paid $500 of employment income with an employment period of 20 days. Jess's income is assessed over 20 days and $25 of employment income is attributed to each day of the assessment period. *Social Security Guide (4.3.3.07)*

Assessing employment income from the first day in the entitlement period in which the amount is paid ensures the payment is applied consistently to the period regardless of which day in the period the payment is received. This would mean that $350 ($25*14) is attributed to the first entitlement period and $150 is attributed to the second entitlement period. As a result, $25 would be attributed to each day in the first entitlement period and $10.71 ($150÷14) would be attributed to each day of the second entitlement period.

Example 2: Lewis is paid $400 from one of his employers which is assessed over 4 weeks ($200 per fortnight). 2 weeks later Lewis is paid $400 from a different employer which is also assessed over 2 weeks.

$600 in total is assigned to the second fortnight where the attribution of the 2 amounts overlaps ($200+$400). *Social Security Guide (4.3.3.07)*

Entitlement period	Attribution calculation	Daily attribution
1	$400÷28 = $14.29 per day $14.29*14 = $200 attributed $200 remaining for attribution into next entitlement period	$14.29
2	Income from employer 1 $200÷14 = $14.29 $0 remaining	$14.29
	Income from employer 2 $400÷14 = $28.57 per day $28.57*14 = $400 attributed for this entitlement period $0 remaining	$28.57

Deferred Income, Salary Sacrifice, Valuable Consideration and Fringe Benefits

When we talk about "employment income," it is easy to assume we are only talking about the cash that hits your bank account every fortnight. But in the eyes of the social security system, the definition is much broader. If you are trying to understand how your real-world earnings impact your benefits, you need to look past the payslip.

The system is designed to capture not just your cash salary, but also those clever arrangements—like salary sacrificing or receiving perks instead of money—that essentially function as income.

When Income Isn't Just Cash

Sometimes, income doesn't look like money at all. We call this "valuable consideration." If your employer gives you something of value—or if they pay for something on your behalf—that is treated as income.

Think of it this way: if you were given a brand-new television as a perk of the job, the system treats that as if you had been paid the cash equivalent to buy it yourself. As the *Social Security Guide (4.3.3.60)* states: *"If an item is given to a person (or their partner), as valuable consideration, the normal cost of purchasing that item IS assessed as income for the 12-month period from the date the item is received."*

For example, if you receive a television, *"the purchase price is assessed as income."* Similarly, if your employer leases or hires an item for your personal use, the cost of that lease or hire is assessed as income for the duration of that agreement.

The Salary Sacrifice Trap

Many people use salary sacrifice—putting money into superannuation before it hits their pocket—to manage their taxes. However, for social security purposes, these arrangements are often treated as income, regardless of the tax benefits.

Since 1 July 2009, any salary or wages that an employee voluntarily sacrifices into superannuation is considered income for social security purposes. The system views this as money you had the power to receive, but chose to direct elsewhere.

The Social Security Guide explains: *"Some employees may engage in superannuation salary sacrifice arrangements where: the employer increases the amount contributed to the employee's superannuation fund, and at the same time the employer reduces the employee's wages by the amount contributed to superannuation." Social Security Guide (4.3.3.60)*

It is important to distinguish this from compulsory employer contributions. If your employer is simply fulfilling their legal obligations under the Superannuation Guarantee, an award, or a workplace agreement, that money is not assessed as your income.

Fringe Benefits: The "Gross-Up" Complexity

Fringe benefits are effectively "perks"—think of things like a company car or health insurance premiums paid by your employer. These are valuable considerations, and if you salary sacrifice into a fringe benefit, it is treated as income.

The tricky part here is the "gross-up" value. Because fringe benefits are not taxed in the same way as your regular salary, the tax office reports them on your payment summary as a "grossed-up" figure—essentially estimating what you would have had to earn in pre-tax dollars to buy that benefit yourself.

However, for social security purposes, they want the real value, not the inflated tax figure. The guideline explains: *"For social security income test purposes the value of the NON-grossed-up fringe benefits IS to be used." Social Security Guide (4.3.3.60)*

If you are looking at a payment summary and seeing a large, confusing "grossed-up" figure, you need to "de-gross" it to find the actual amount that affects your payments. The formula provided in the guide is: *"non-grossed-up fringe benefits = grossed-up value of benefits * (1 – FBT rate)."*

To give you a real-world example from the official records: *"For the FBT year ending 31 March 2023, John has received fringe benefits from his employer. The amounts which will be shown on the payment summary for the financial year ending 30 June 2023 are $3,883.50 and $5,825.24, giving a total reportable amount of $9,708.74. To determine the adjusted fringe benefits total apply the previously mentioned formula: Reportable fringe benefits amount * (1 – FBT rate). $9,708.74 * (1 – 0.47) = $5,145.63."*
Note: This example is extracted from Social Security Guide

In this case, the $5,145.63 is the actual amount that is taken into account under the income test, not the much higher figure that might appear on a tax document.

A Note on Deferred Income

Finally, what happens if your pay is delayed? If you have no choice in the matter—say, a workplace agreement dictates you cannot receive certain payments until you leave the company or take leave—then that income is generally not assessed until you actually receive it. As the guidelines note: *"If there was a change to the award and the employee could not receive the income until they resigned or until they took leave in the future, income is not assessed until the employee leaves the job or takes the leave."*

The social security system is designed to assess the actual economic value of a recipient's remuneration, regardless of the technical labels or structures used. Because non-cash benefits and sacrificed salary have specific assessment rules, verifying their classification helps maintain accurate reporting.

Chapter 10: The Work Bonus — Keeping More of What You Earn

If you've reached Age Pension age, you might be thinking about staying in the workforce—whether that's keeping your current job, picking up some part-time consulting, or starting a small business. A common worry is that working will simply lead to a reduction in your pension. This is where the Work Bonus comes into play. It's designed to be an incentive, allowing you to earn more from your efforts without it hitting your pension as hard as "ordinary" income.

What is the Work Bonus?

The Work Bonus is essentially a "discount" on your employment income. For every fortnight, the first $300 of your income from work is completely disregarded for the pension income test.

If you don't earn $300 in a particular fortnight, you don't lose that benefit. Instead, the "unused" portion of that $300 is banked into your Work Bonus Income Bank. This bank can grow up to a maximum of $11,800. Think of this bank as a reserve you can draw upon later; if you have a big-earning month, you can use these banked credits to offset that income and keep your pension intact.

The "Starting Bonus"

When you first claim an eligible payment, you don't start with an empty tank. To give you an immediate boost, the government provides a one-off $4,000 credit to your Work Bonus bank the moment your pension is granted.

Who is Eligible and How Does it Apply?

You are eligible for the Work Bonus if you have reached Age Pension age and receive an eligible payment, such as the Age Pension, Carer Payment, or Disability Support Pension.

It's crucial to understand that the Work Bonus is strictly an individual benefit. While the department assesses couples as a financial unit for the income test, the Work Bonus itself cannot be shared.

- If you are the only one working: You can use your own $300 fortnightly concession and your own banked credits to offset your earnings.
- If your partner is the only one working: If your partner is under Age Pension age, they are not eligible for the Work Bonus. Consequently, their employment income is treated as ordinary income and will be assessed at its full value. You cannot "transfer" or "gift" your Work Bonus balance to your partner to offset their earnings.

Do You Need to Apply?

The best news is that you don't need to fill out any forms or formally apply. The system is automatic. As long as you keep the department updated on your income—by reporting your earnings through your online account—the department will apply the Work Bonus and draw from your income bank whenever it's to your advantage.

Examples

Example 1: The Single Pensioner (Drawing from the Bank) *Arthur is an Age Pensioner who works as a freelance bookkeeper.*

- Situation: Arthur has a total of $5,000 in his Work Bonus Bank (which includes his initial $4,000 starting bonus plus accrued credits). This month, he picks up a large contract and earns $1,200 in a single fortnight.
- Calculation:
    1. The standard $300 fortnightly concession is applied ($1,200 - $300 = $900 remaining).
    2. The remaining $900 is offset using his banked credits.

3. Because he has $5,000 in his bank, the entire $900 is wiped out for the income test.

- Result: Arthur's assessable income for this fortnight is $0. He keeps his pension unchanged, and his Work Bonus Bank balance is now $4,100 ($5,000 - $900).

Example 2: The Working Partner (Under Age Pension Age) *Barbara is 65 and John is 67 (receiving the Age Pension).*

- Situation: They are a couple. John is retired, but Barbara is working part-time, earning $600 per fortnight.
- Calculation:
    1. Because Barbara is under Age Pension age, she is not eligible for the Work Bonus.
    2. The full $600 of her employment income is counted as assessable income for the couple's combined pension assessment.
    3. John's Work Bonus Bank cannot be used to offset Barbara's earnings.

- Result: The couple's combined assessable income increases by the full $600. Even though John is an eligible pensioner, the Work Bonus is locked to his individual earnings and cannot be applied to his partner's wages.

Because banked Work Bonus credits do not expire and can carry over indefinitely, they allow recipients to balance temporary workforce earnings with their ongoing pension entitlement. Since the Work Bonus is an individual concession, any accrued credit remains strictly tied to the individual who earned the income and cannot be transferred to a partner.

Chapter 11: Income from Boarders and Lodgers

If you have a spare room in your house, you might have considered bringing in a boarder or a lodger to help with the household expenses. It's a practical way to manage costs, but when it comes to social security payments, the rules can feel a little complex. It's important to understand how this extra cash is treated so you don't get caught off guard during an income assessment.

The "Family" Exception

First, let's clear up a very important distinction. If you provide accommodation to an immediate family member—specifically your parents, your children, or your siblings—this arrangement is not counted as income for social security purposes. The government recognises that supporting family is a private matter, and they don't look at money exchanged within that circle in the same way they view a commercial arrangement.

How It Works for Everyone Else

When you start renting out a room to anyone outside of that immediate family circle, the rules shift. The government assumes that a portion of the money you receive is covering the costs of providing that accommodation, and only the remaining portion is counted as "income" for your payment assessment.

The amount they count as income depends on the type of arrangement you have:

- Lodging (Accommodation only): They assess 70% of the money you receive as income.
- Bed and Breakfast (Accommodation + breakfast): They assess 50% of the money you receive.
- Board (Accommodation + meals in addition to breakfast): They assess 20% of the money you receive.

A simple example: If you own your house outright and rent a room to a lodger for $200 per week:

- You receive $10,400 per year ($200 × 52 weeks).
- The government assesses 70% of that as income, which is $7,280 per year.

Can You Reduce the Assessed Amount?

Yes, in certain situations, you can lower the amount that gets counted against your benefits.

1. If you have a mortgage: You can deduct the annual interest on the mortgage for your home from your assessable income.

   - *Example:* A single person receives $200 per week for accommodation and breakfast ($10,400/year). The assessable 50% is $5,200. If they have a $100,000 mortgage at 6% interest, that is an interest cost of $6,000 per year. Because the interest ($6,000) is higher than the assessed income ($5,200), the assessable income is NIL.

2. If you are a renter: If you are renting your own principal residence and taking in a boarder, you can deduct the rent you pay from the income you receive.

- *Example:* A single person receives $200 per week for full board ($10,400/year). The assessable 20% is $2,080. If they are paying $210 per week in rent ($10,920/year), the rent paid is higher than the assessable income, so the result is NIL.

A Few Final Points

- Reassessment: If you feel these standard percentages don't reflect your actual costs—perhaps you are spending significantly more on electricity or heating—you can request a reassessment. You will need to provide concrete evidence of these higher expenses, as the authorities will need to investigate before applying any changes.

- Commercial Operations: If you move from having a spare room to letting out more than five rooms, the arrangement is considered a commercial venture, and the government will look at your net profit rather than these percentage-based calculations.
- Fluctuating Income: If your income varies because rooms are often vacant, the government may choose to accept the net profit figure from your latest tax return instead of the standard percentages.

Understanding the specific percentages and thresholds applied to boarder and lodger arrangements is a key component of household budgeting. Knowing how the system assesses this income allows residents to anticipate the exact impact on their pension before finalising a tenancy agreement.

Chapter 12: Income from Real Estate (Beyond the Family Home)

In the last chapter, we talked about boarders and lodgers—the people you might share your own roof with. But what if you own a rental property? Perhaps you've bought an investment apartment, inherited a house, or moved into a new home and decided to keep your old one to rent out.

When you start earning rent from property that *isn't* your principal place of residence, the assessment rules change significantly. Unlike the "boarder" rules, which rely on simple percentages, assessing rental income is all about your "net" income.

The Core Principle: Net Income

For social security purposes, the authorities aren't interested in the "gross" rent—the total amount of money that lands in your bank account from the tenant. They are interested in your net income. Essentially, the government wants to know what you are actually walking away with after the necessary costs of maintaining that property are paid.

Generally speaking, if you've already filed a tax return, the government will use your tax figures as the baseline. The deductions they allow for your pension or payment assessment mirror the deductions allowed by the ATO (Australian Taxation Office), but with a few very specific, important differences.

What You Can Deduct

When calculating your assessable income, you are allowed to subtract the necessary costs of running the rental property. This typically includes:

- Costs to maintain the property
- Rates.
- Loan interest payments.

A crucial warning on mortgages: If you took out a loan to buy a new "principal home," and you used your old home as collateral to secure that loan, the interest on that loan is not an allowable deduction. The government views the dominant purpose of that loan as buying a personal home, not an investment property.

What You *Cannot* Deduct

There are certain expenses that the ATO might let you claim for tax purposes that the social security system does not recognise:

- Capital depreciation.
- "Special building write-offs" or construction costs.
- Borrowing costs (like loan establishment fees).

Also, keep in mind that you cannot "double dip." If you have two rental properties and one is running at a loss, you cannot use that loss to offset the income from your profitable property. If a property is running at a net loss, for social security purposes, your income from that specific property is simply recorded as NIL.

Estimating Deductions (When you don't have a tax return)

If you've only just started renting out a property and don't have a tax return to show yet, you don't have to guess wildly. You can use an estimation method:

- Start with the gross rent received.
- Deduct one-third of that amount (this acts as a "blanket" deduction to cover your rates, insurance, repairs, and other standard costs).
- Deduct your mortgage interest payments from the remaining balance.

Note: If you find that your actual costs are significantly higher than that one-third estimate—perhaps because the property needed a lot of work to become habitable—you can provide evidence of those actual expenses instead. However, this doesn't include "improvements" or structural alterations, which are considered capital investments rather than ongoing costs.

Chapter 13: Earning as a Sole Trader or in a Partnership

If you've decided to be your own boss, whether that's running a small business as a sole trader or working in partnership with others, your income journey becomes a little different from the standard "paycheck" model. When you're self-employed, you don't get a neat summary at the end of the year from an employer; instead, you're the one responsible for tracking what's coming in and what's going out.

When it comes to your social security payments, the government doesn't look at your "turnover"—the total amount of cash that flows through your business. They are interested in your net income.

How Your Income is Assessed

The golden rule here is that your income for payment assessment is based on the net profit of your business.

This is your gross income minus the allowable business expenses you’ve incurred to earn that money.

Usually, the department will look at your most recent tax return to determine your net profit. They take the figure you reported to the Australian Taxation Office (ATO) and use that as the starting point for your benefit assessment. However, it’s not always a mirror image of your tax return. There are some specific rules they apply to ensure their assessment aligns with their own policies.

The "Assessment" Difference

While the Australian Taxation Office and Services Australia often use similar figures, they don't always agree on what constitutes an "allowable" deduction. For instance:

- Adjustments: Sometimes, the government may need to "add back" certain deductions that you’ve claimed for tax purposes (superannuation contributions for the sole trader or partner of the partnership) because the sole trader or partner of the partnership is not considered to be an employee. However, superannuation contributions to employees are allowable.

What if You're Just Starting Out?

If you've recently launched your venture and don't have a tax return yet, don't worry. You won't be expected to have a year's worth of history. In these cases, you'll be asked to provide an estimate of your income.

You'll need to put together a projection of your expected gross income and subtract your expected business-related costs. It helps to be as realistic as possible here. If your business takes a turn and your income ends up being significantly different from your initial estimate, you have a duty to update the department. Maintaining detailed business diaries or financial spreadsheets helps sole traders track these variations and provide accurate, up-to-date projections to the department.

The Reality of Partnerships

If you are in a partnership, the rules are fairly straightforward: the income is assessed based on your share of the net profit of the partnership. Even if the money stays in the business account and isn't physically transferred to your personal bank account, for the purposes of your payment assessment, that profit is still considered yours.

A Final Piece of Advice

Being a sole trader is rewarding, but the paperwork can be the most challenging part. Keeping business financial transactions separate from personal spending simplifies end-of-year tax filing and administrative reviews. Utilising a dedicated business bank account provides a clear, auditable trail that demonstrates the exact net profit of the business to the department during any review processes.

For businesses with high expenses or complex operating structures, retaining receipts and detailed records is crucial for verifying "allowable" deductions. Systematic record-keeping ensures that the means test assessment is based accurately on the business's true net profit.

Chapter 14: Understanding Deeming

When you're navigating the pension or income support system, one of the most common points of confusion is how the government calculates the "income" from your savings and investments. Rather than tracking every cent of interest you earn from a high-interest savings account or every dividend from your share portfolio, the government uses a simplified method called deeming.

What Is Deeming?

Think of deeming as a way for the government to "estimate" the income your financial assets generate. Instead of looking at your actual bank statements to see what you earned, the system assumes your money is earning a specific rate of return, regardless of what that money is *actually* doing in your account.

The Big Advantage

The primary benefit of deeming is simplicity and fairness. If you are a savvy investor who finds an account paying 5% interest, you aren't penalised for your financial skill—the government still only counts the "deemed" rate as your income. Conversely, if your money is sitting in a low-interest account, the government assumes it could be earning more, so they calculate your income based on that expected rate. This encourages people to seek out reasonable returns without being punished for doing well.

How Deemed Income Is Calculated

Calculating your deemed income is a two-tier process based on the total value of your financial assets. As of July 2026, the rates are:

- The Low Rate (1.25%): This is applied to the first portion of your assets.
- The High Rate (3.25%): This is applied to any balance above the initial threshold.

If your actual investment returns are higher than the deeming rates, the additional return is not separately assessed as income.

Deeming Thresholds by Marital Status

The thresholds change depending on your relationship status, recognising that couples often pool their resources.

Status	Low Rate Threshold (at 1.25%)	High Rate Threshold (at 3.25%)
Single	First $66,800	Above $66,800
Couple (Combined)	First $110,600	Above $110,600

Note: These figures are current and valid as at July 2026.

Practical Examples: Putting It All Together

Deeming doesn't just apply to cash in the bank. It covers most financial investments, including listed shares, managed funds, and money held in superannuation accumulation accounts once you have reached pension age.

Note: Assets like your account-based pension are also subject to deeming, as are most other financial investments.

Example 1: The Single Investor

Sarah has a diverse portfolio: $40,000 in a savings account, $30,000 in a managed fund, and $30,000 in shares, for a total of $100,000 in financial assets.

- First $66,800: $66,800 × 1.25% = $835
- Remaining $33,200 ($100,000 - $66,800): $33,200 × 3.25% = $1,079
- Total Annual Deemed Income: $1,914

Example 2: The Retired Couple

John and Mary have a combined portfolio: $50,000 in a super accumulation account, $100,000 in an account-based pension, and $50,000 in shares/managed funds, totalling $200,000 in financial assets.

- First $110,600: $110,600 × 1.25% = $1,382.50
- Remaining $89,400 ($200,000 - $110,600): $89,400 × 3.25% = $2,905.50
- Total Annual Deemed Income: $4,288.00

As you can see, the specific type of investment matters less than the total value. Whether that money is in a bank, a share portfolio, or a superannuation account, it all gets added to the same "deeming bucket." It's a predictable system that, once understood, makes it much easier to estimate your own fortnightly pension entitlement.

Chapter 15: Understanding Your Assets

While the income test tracks the money flowing into your pocket, the assets test looks at your "stockpile"—the total value of what you own. To determine if you're eligible for a pension, the government adds up all your assets. If the total exceeds specific thresholds, your pension may be reduced.

For assessment purposes, your holdings are split into two main groups: financial assets and non-financial assets.

- Financial Assets: These are your liquid or semi-liquid holdings. They include bank accounts, term deposits, shares, managed investments, superannuation (once you reach Age Pension age), and even cash on hand.

- Non-Financial Assets: This category covers your physical possessions, such as your vehicle, caravan, boat, furniture, electronics, jewellery, and hobby collections. These are assessed based on their current market value—essentially, what a willing buyer would pay for them in their current second-hand condition.

Gifting

You are free to give away your money or property whenever you choose, but if you want to protect your pension, you need to be aware of the "gifting" or "deprivation" rules. If you give away an asset for less than its market value without receiving adequate payment in return, the department may count that gift as a "deprived asset."

The Limits: To remain within the "gifting-free" area, you (or you and your partner combined) can gift:

- Up to $10,000 in a single financial year.
- No more than $30,000 over a rolling five-year period.

What happens if you exceed these limits? If you gift more than these amounts, the excess is treated as a deprived asset for five years from the date of the gift. This means:

- The excess amount is added to your total assessable assets.
- The excess amount is "deemed" to earn income.

Essentially, the department acts as if you still own that money for five years. After the five-year period has passed, the gift "drops off" and no longer affects your assessment. Due to the strict nature of the deprivation rules and the complexity of calculating overlapping gifts over a rolling five-year period, verifying the historical gift register with the department is a common step taken before making a significant asset transfer.

Loans

Sometimes, you might lend money to a family member, a friend, or an organisation. From the government's perspective, money you have loaned out remains your asset regardless of when the loan was made.

Because you are the "lender," this money is considered a financial investment. Even though the cash is physically sitting in someone else's account or being used for someone else's benefit, the law treats it as your asset.

Consequently, these loans are subject to the same deeming rules as your bank accounts. This means the department will assume your "loaned" money is earning interest at the standard deeming rates, regardless of whether you are actually charging interest or receiving any repayments.

Failed Loans

A failed loan is a loan that is not performing to the terms of the loan agreement and it is usually accepted as "failed" when legal recovery action has been, or is, being taken. The case may then be referred to a Complex Assessment Office (CAO) for assessment. If you find yourself in this situation, you will need to provide evidence, such as reports from an insolvency practitioner or court documents, to prove the money is genuinely gone.

Insurance Bonds and Life Insurance Policies

Life insurance and investment-style insurance products are handled with a bit more complexity because they often serve a dual purpose: providing a safety net and acting as an investment vehicle.

- Insurance Bonds: These are considered financial investments. If your bond is held in units, its assessable value is the number of units you own multiplied by the current value per unit. If the bond is account-based, the assessable value is simply your current account balance. Because these are financial investments, they are subject to the deeming rules. It is worth noting that the value of these bonds can fluctuate, so the value you see on your statement may differ from your initial purchase price.

- Life Insurance Policies: Only policies with an investment component are assessable as an asset. Products such as term insurance, disability, trauma or income protection insurance do not have a surrender value—the amount you would receive if you ended the policy today, so have a nil value for assets test purposes. The assessable value of a person's life insurance policy is the surrender value.

Chapter 16: The Assets Test and Real Estate

In our last chapter, we established that the assets test measures the "stockpile" of everything you own. While financial assets and personal possessions are fairly straightforward, real estate is often the most significant—and complex—part of the calculation. When you own property beyond your own four walls, the department views it through a specific lens: what is its net value?

The Principal Home: Your "Safe" Asset

The home you live in as your principal residence is generally exempt from the assets test. This ensures that your housing security is protected. However, this exemption is not a blanket rule; it is tied to how you occupy and use that land.

The 2-Hectare Rule

Your home is exempt, along with any land on the same title up to 2 hectares (roughly 5 acres). If your property is larger than 2 hectares, the value of the "excess" land is counted as an assessable asset.

The Exception

If you have lived on the property for at least 20 years and are making "effective use" of the land to earn a living, you may apply for an extended land use exemption, which could keep the larger block exempt.

Business Use

If you use a portion of your principal home *solely* for business purposes—such as a dedicated office, a professional studio, or a workshop that isn't used for domestic living—that specific portion of your property is no longer exempt. It will be carved out and assessed as an asset according to its market value.

Self-Contained Areas

Similarly, if you have a separate, self-contained living area on your property, it is usually considered part of your principal home—meaning it remains exempt. However, if you rent that self-contained area to someone other than a near relative (like a parent, child, or sibling), that portion of the property is treated as an assessable asset, and the rental income is assessed under the income test.

Assessable Real Estate

Any property that is not your principal home is considered an assessable asset. This includes holiday homes, investment properties, vacant land, and commercial buildings.

Valuation

For these properties, the department uses the current market value for the assets test. This is the price you could reasonably expect to get if you sold the property on the open market today. You do not need to provide a professional valuation every single year, but you must provide a realistic estimate.

Net Equity

You aren't penalised for the full value of the property if you owe money on it. Generally, a debt secured against the property can be deducted from its market value, so the assessable value may be based on the property's net value rather than its full market value.

Retirement Villages

If you move into a retirement village, your "homeowner" status is determined by your Entry Contribution (the lump sum you pay to secure your unit).

Extra Allowable Amount

Definition: the difference between homeowner and non-homeowner assets test limits, at the time the person enters the special residence.

Homeowner Status

- If you pay more than the "extra allowable amount": You are classified as a homeowner. This is beneficial because your entry contribution is exempt from the assets test, just like a traditional family home.
- If you pay equal to or less than "extra allowable amount": You are classified as a non-homeowner. While this means your entry contribution *is* counted as an asset, you may qualify for higher assets-test thresholds that apply to non-homeowners.

Granny Flat Interest

What Is A Granny Flat Interest?

A "granny flat interest" is a specific legal arrangement where you pay money or transfer assets to another person in exchange for the right to live in a property for the rest of your life.

You are not considered to have paid more than the interest is worth (and thus avoid "deprivation" or gifting penalties) if you:

- Transfer the title of your home and keep a lifetime right to live there or in another property.
- Pay to build a granny flat on someone else's property.
- Pay to convert someone else's home to suit your needs and receive a lifetime right to live there.
- Buy a property in someone else's name while retaining a lifetime right to live there.

Homeowner Status

When you establish a granny flat interest, the department determines your status by comparing the amount you paid (your Entry Contribution) against the Extra Allowable Amount (EAA):

- If your Entry Contribution is greater than the EAA: You are classified as a homeowner. Your Entry Contribution is exempt from the assets test, and you are treated as if you still own your own home.
- If your Entry Contribution is equal to or less than EAA: You are classified as a non-homeowner. Your Entry Contribution is counted as an assessable asset, but you may qualify for the higher "non-homeowner" assets-test thresholds.

The Reasonableness Test

Generally, the value of your granny flat interest is simply the amount you paid for it, meaning no gifting occurs. However, the department applies a Reasonableness Test to ensure the arrangement isn't being used to artificially shield assets from the means tests.

The government uses the reasonableness test when you have:

- Transferred extra assets in addition to the granny flat arrangement.
- Made a lump sum contribution towards existing accommodation at someone else's property where no construction or renovations have occurred.

The reasonableness test uses a formula to calculate "reasonable amount" and

- If the amount you paid is higher than this "reasonable" calculated amount, the department may treat the difference as a gift (a deprived asset). This excess amount would then be counted as an asset for five years, and the deeming rules would apply to it.
- If your payment is less than or equal to the reasonable amount, your interest is valued at the amount paid, and no gifting occurs.

Summary Checklist for Your Records

Maintaining an updated file for each owned property helps ensure means test assessments remain accurate. Relevant documentation includes:

- Your latest council rates notice (which often contains a valuation).
- Any recent real estate appraisals or sale contracts for similar properties in your area.
- Your latest mortgage statement showing the remaining balance.
- If you've rented out a self-contained area or use part of your home for a business, records clearly defining that space.

Having these documents ready makes it incredibly easy to update the department if your property situation changes, ensuring you are neither over-assessed nor under-paid.

Chapter 17: Superannuation and the Means Tests

When you're planning for retirement, superannuation often feels like a "locked box" until you reach a certain age. However, when you become a pensioner, that box becomes a significant part of your financial profile in the eyes of the government. Understanding how the department views your super is essential for managing your overall benefit entitlement.

What is Superannuation?

At its core, superannuation is a long-term savings vehicle designed to fund your life after you stop working. During your "accumulation phase," your employer (and potentially you) makes contributions which are invested by a fund trustee. The goal is to grow these savings through investment returns so that, eventually, you can draw on them as a lump sum, a pension (income stream), or a combination of both.

Types of Superannuation Funds or Schemes

While many people just see "their super," the underlying structure can vary. Generally, these funds fall into two main categories:

- Accumulation or Defined Contribution Funds: This is the most common type for the modern workforce. Your final benefit is simply the total of the contributions made by you and your employer, plus whatever investment returns the fund has generated. The "size" of your final nest egg depends entirely on how well these investments perform over time.
- Defined Benefit Funds: These are often found in older corporate schemes or the public sector. Instead of a balance that fluctuates with market performance, your benefit is calculated using a specific formula—usually involving your final salary (or an average of your last few years of service) multiplied by your length of

membership and a percentage of final salary for each year of service. In these schemes, the employer is responsible for contributing whatever is necessary to meet the fund's obligations to its members.

Beyond these two structural types, your super might be held in a Public Sector fund (for government employees), a Corporate fund (for employees of specific large companies), an Industry fund (multi-employer funds), or a Self-Managed Superannuation Fund (SMSF), where you personally act as the trustee for your own retirement savings.

How is Superannuation Assessed?

The way your super is assessed depends largely on your age.

- If you are under Age Pension age: Superannuation that remains in the accumulation phase is generally not counted as an asset for the pension means tests.

- If you have reached Age Pension age: The rules change. From the moment you reach Age Pension age, your superannuation becomes an assessable asset. It is treated as a financial investment, meaning it is subject to the deeming rules. Regardless of the actual earnings or dividends the fund reports, the department will apply the standard deeming rates to the balance.

Withdrawing Your Super

Many people worry that withdrawing a lump sum from their super will "ruin" their pension. It's important to understand that withdrawing your own money doesn't mean you've lost it; you've simply moved it from one "bucket" (the super fund) to another (your bank account).

- Lump Sums: If you take a lump sum withdrawal, the money enters your personal bank account. It remains a financial asset, and it remains subject to the deeming rules. The only real change is *where* it is held.

- Income Streams (Pensions): If you convert your super into an account-based pension, that pension is also treated as a financial asset and is subject to deeming. For older, non-account-based income streams, the assessment can be more complex.

Chapter 18: Income Streams

As you move into retirement, you may convert your superannuation or other savings into an "income stream." These are financial products that provide regular income payments throughout retirement. Because these products effectively turn your capital into a regular payment, the government applies specific assessment rules that vary based on the type of product and, crucially, when you purchased it.

Account-Based Pensions

These are the most common income streams. You move your super into an account where it remains invested, and you draw a regular payment.

Asset Assessment

The full account balance is counted as an assessable asset.

Income Assessment

- Purchased on or after 1 January 2015: Subject to standard deeming rules. The actual amount you withdraw is ignored; instead, the government applies the deeming rules to your account balance rather than assessing the actual withdrawals.
- Purchased before 1 January 2015 (Grandfathered): If you held the pension and were receiving an income support payment before this date, and have remained in continuous receipt of an income support payment since, your assessable income is the gross annual payment received minus a "deductible amount" [(purchase price - residual capital value) ÷ relevant number]. If that continuous entitlement is broken, the grandfathering provisions cease and the income stream becomes subject to deeming.

Note: In the case of account-based income streams, the residual capital value is generally zero.

Lifetime Income Streams

These products provide a guaranteed income for life. The rules for these have changed significantly over time, creating different "classes" of products depending on when you bought them.

Purchased on or after 1 July 2019

Asset Assessment

Generally 60% of the purchase price is counted as an assessable asset until you reach your "threshold day". After this day, only 30% of the purchase price is assessed for the rest of your life.

Note: The threshold day is the later of:

- *the day you reach age 84, or*
- *5 years after the commencement date*

Income Assessment

Only 60% of the gross payments you receive are counted as assessable income.

Purchased on or after 20 September 2007 and before 1 July 2019

These do not qualify for the newer 60%/30% concessions. They are generally assessed under the "asset-tested long-term" rules.

Asset Assessment

Fully assessed using formula:
Purchase price – [((purchase price – RCV) ÷ relevant number) × term elapsed]

Income Assessment

The gross payment minus the deductible amount.

Purchased on or after 20 September 2004 and before 20 September 2007

Asset Assessment

These are eligible for a 50% assets test exemption, provided they comply with section 9A.

Income Assessment

The gross payment minus the deductible amount.

Purchased before 20 September 2004

Asset Assessment

These are eligible for a 100% assets test exemption, provided they comply with section 9A.

Income Assessment

The gross payment minus the deductible amount.

Defined Benefit Income Streams

These are provided by older corporate or public sector schemes. Your payment is determined by a formula based on your salary and length of service.

Asset Assessment

Generally exempt from the assets test.

Income Assessment

The gross annual payment minus a "deductible amount." Since 1 January 2016, the deductible amount is capped at 10% of the gross payment.

Note: The deductible amount is generally based on the tax-free component determined by the superannuation provider. Not all defined benefit income streams will have a tax-free component.

Market-Linked Income Streams (Term Allocated Pensions)

Market-linked income stream (MLI), also known as Term Allocated Pension, was introduced on 20 September 2004. This product is not an account-based income stream nor is it a life expectancy income stream. MLIs are like account-based income streams in that they are account-based products where the value of the account balance moves up or down in line with the value of the underlying assets. They are also like life expectancy income streams with payments being paid for a fixed term.

Asset Assessment

MLIs must meet all the characteristics needed under section 9BA of the Social Security Act 1991 to be 50% assets-test exempt. Purchased on or after 20 September 2007, the income stream is fully assessable as an asset.

Income Assessment

The gross annual payment minus a "deductible amount."

References

Chapter 1	Social Security Guide 3.1.1.10
Chapter 2	Social Security Guide 2.2.5.30 Services Australia Website Search for QC 50091
Chapter 3	Social Security Guide 4.6.3.20
Chapter 4	Social Security Guide 4.6.3.30, 4.6.3.60
Chapter 5	Services Australia Website Search for QC 43696, QC 51757
Chapter 6	Social Security Guide 4.6.8.50 Services Australia Website Search for QC 27571
Chapter 7	Services Australia Website Search for QC 30376, QC 28961, QC 30621, QC 28486
Chapter 8	Services Australia Website Search for QC 25326
Chapter 9	Social Security Guide 4.3.3.05, 4.3.3.06, 4.3.3.07, 4.3.3.60
Chapter 10	Social Security Guide 3.1.15.20

Chapter 11	Social Security Guide 4.3.8.40
Chapter 12	Services Australia Website Search for QC 28966
Chapter 13	Social Security Guide 4.7.1.20
Chapter 14	Services Australia Website Search for QC 29656
Chapter 15	Social Security Guide 4.6.5.60, 4.6.5.70
Chapter 16	Services Australia Website Search for QC 30731
Chapter 17	Social Security Guide 4.8.1.20
Chapter 18	Social Security Guide 4.9.2